30119 026 176 94 3

LIFE DIS
SOA

THE MATT MERTON
MYSTERIES

THE WARNING

Paul Blum

D1375348

RISING★STARS

LONDON BOROUGH OF SUTTON LIBRARY SERVICE (SUT)	
30119 026 176 94 3	
Askews	Dec-2010
JF	

nasen
Helping Everyone Achieve
■ ■ ■ nasen

NASEN House, 4/5 Amber Business Village, Amber Close,
Amington, Tamworth, Staffordshire B77 4RP

Rising Stars UK Ltd.
22 Grafton Street, London W1S 4EX
www.risingstars-uk.com

Text © Rising Stars UK Ltd.
The right of Paul Blum to be identified as the author of this work has
been asserted by him in accordance with the Copyright, Design and
Patents Act, 1988.

Published 2010

Cover design: pentacorbig
Illustrator: Chris King, Illustration Ltd
Photos: Alamy
Text design and typesetting: pentacorbig/Clive Sutherland
Publisher: Gill Budgell
Editorial consultants: Lorraine Petersen and Dee Reid

All rights reserved. No part of this publication may be reproduced, stored
in a retrieval system or transmitted in any form by any means, electronic,
mechanical, photocopying, recording or otherwise without the prior
permission of Rising Stars UK Ltd.

British Library Cataloguing in Publication Data.
A CIP record for this book is available from the British Library.

ISBN: 978-1-84680-795-4

Printed by Craft Print International Limited, Singapore

THE MATT MERTON
MYSTERIES

CONTENTS

THE CRASH

The Crash happened in 2021. Alien spaceships crash-landed on Earth. Now the aliens rule the world. They have changed shape so they look like people. People call the aliens The Enemy. Since The Crash, people are afraid. They don't know who is an Enemy and who is a friend.

An organisation called The Firm keeps order on the streets. The Firm keeps people safe from Enemy attacks — or do they?

People are going missing and the Earth is becoming colder and darker all the time. A new ice age is coming ...

ABOUT MATT MERTON

Matt Merton works for The Firm. He often works with **Dexter**. Their job is to find and kill The Enemy. They use Truth Sticks to do this.

But Matt has problems. He has lost some of his memory and cannot answer some big questions.

Where has **Jane**, his girlfriend, gone?

How did he get his job with **The Firm**?

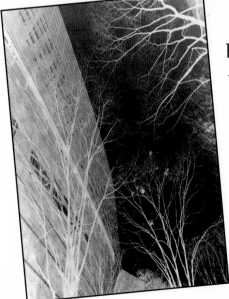

Matt thinks The Firm is on the side of good. But he is not sure …

CHAPTER 1

Matt Merton's boss was not a happy man. There had been another attack on the city. The Enemy had been leaving bombs in the sky trains and people were scared. The Firm had to find The Enemy and they had to find them quickly. But they had no idea where they were.

Then The Firm got a lead. The Enemy were hiding in a seaside town. They had a bomb-making factory in a little house on the coast.

Matt Merton's boss sent him an email about it early one morning.

I want you and Dexter to go to the coast. The Enemy are hiding there. You must find and destroy them.

Matt rubbed his eyes. 'Just time to get a coffee at Sam's cafe,' he said to himself.

'What are you having today?' asked Sam.

'Just a coffee. Extra hot with an extra shot,' said Matt.

'Do you want that to go?' asked Sam.

Matt looked at his watch. 'No, I'll have it here,' he said. 'I need to be wide awake to deal with Dexter.'

Matt and Dexter often worked together, but they didn't like each other.

They drove out of the city in silence.

Dexter had a smile on his face. He liked to tease Matt. Dexter broke the silence.

'So Merton, any news about that missing girlfriend of yours? What was her name ... Tina, wasn't it?'

Matt looked out of the window. 'It's Jane, not Tina, ' he said.

Dexter laughed. 'Tina, Jane, whatever,' he said. 'She's been gone for months. You shouldn't let yourself get so worked up about her.'

Matt said nothing.

'Take my advice, partner,' said Dexter.

'I don't want your advice,' Matt replied. 'And you're not my partner.'

But Dexter was just warming up. 'You should forget about her and move on.'

Matt didn't reply. He was too angry. Anyway, he had his own plan for finding Jane.

Matt tried to change the subject.

'I love the sea,' said Matt. 'I think I came here on holiday when I was a kid.'

Dexter just laughed at him. 'Matt, you aren't a kid anymore. This isn't a holiday, it's work. Grow up.'

Matt said nothing. He didn't care what Dexter thought of him.

He looked out of the window. The sky was grey. The
clouds were heavy with snow. Since The Crash, it was
always winter and never summer. Since The Crash, he
found it hard to think of a reason for living. Every day,
Matt wished he could leave The Firm.

'This is an important job today,' said Dexter. 'There are lots of The Enemy out there to kill.'

Matt sighed. 'Every day has an important job,' he said to himself. 'But I'm sick of all this killing.'

CHAPTER 2

Dexter and Matt went to every house in the small town by the sea. They asked questions. They took photos. But the people did not want to speak to them. There was fear in their eyes.

Matt felt bad. He stood back and Dexter took the lead. Dexter pushed people up against walls and held the Truth Stick up to their faces.

'What's your mother's name?' he shouted at one woman. 'Don't even think about lying to me. You should never lie to The Firm!'

'Stop treating them like that,' said Matt.

'Well, what are they hiding?' said Dexter. 'I'll beat the truth out of them if I have to.'

'Just leave them alone,' said Matt.

But Dexter was angry. He wouldn't let it go.

'Come on, Merton. This place is odd. Something isn't right. The Enemy must be hiding here, ' he said.

'Why must they be hiding here?' asked Matt. 'Just because The Firm got some random tip off? Why do you always think the worst of everybody?'

'It's my job to think the worst. That's the way I catch the bad guys …' started Dexter.

'… and keep the world safe,' finished Matt. 'Yeah, yeah, I know the script.'

Dexter turned on him. 'You may know it but you don't act on it. You're a coward and a traitor.'

'No, I'm not,' said Matt. 'It's clear there is nothing going on here. These people are scared of us. The Firm makes people afraid even if they have nothing to hide. Let's leave them alone. All they want is to lead a quiet life.'

Matt turned and walked away.

'Come back and do your job,' shouted Dexter, 'or you'll be sorry.'

'Do it on your own. I'm done here,' said Matt.

'Get back here now,' said Dexter. 'The Firm are expecting results.'

But Matt had turned his back. He was walking away and he wasn't coming back. The only reason for Matt to stay in The Firm was to use their spies to find Jane. He knew they were tracking her and they were getting close. He just had to hold on a little bit longer.

Dexter was very angry. He called The Firm and shouted down the phone. 'Send me some back-up. Matt Merton has gone mad. He's run out on me. Get everybody here now. We're going with Plan B.'

While Dexter went back to work, Matt skimmed stones on the sea as the snow fell.

The ice on the ground was thicker than ever. A new ice age was coming. Matt could feel it in his bones.

'I can't go on like this. I must leave The Firm before it's too late,' he said to himself. 'They'll find Jane soon. I'll just have to hack into their files and get to her before they do.'

CHAPTER 3

Matt went back to his hotel and went to bed. He fell into a restless sleep but then woke up in the middle of the night. Something wasn't right. He got dressed and walked down to the beach.

As Matt got closer to the beach he could see lots of lights. All the people from the town were there. They were lined up on the sand. Dexter and others from The Firm were standing in front of them.

Dexter put up his hand. At once, all those from The Firm raised their Truth Sticks.

They asked no questions.

They killed everyone.

Matt saw it all. He was shocked. He wanted to shout at them to stop but he felt too dizzy. His legs gave way and he had no voice.

After the mass murder, there was complete silence. Everyone seemed to be waiting for something to happen. All Matt could hear was the beating of his own heart. He couldn't move.

Then, a tall man stepped out from the darkness. He was dressed all in black. He didn't seem to feel the cold. He looked at the pile of ashes on the beach and smiled.

'You have done well. This is just a warning,' he said. 'We will kill The Enemy. We will kill anyone who hides them from us. We will not stop until every one of them is dead and this planet is ours.'

Matt saw the man change. He was not human. He was an alien. Matt gasped in horror as he watched Dexter and the others kneel down in front of him. They were working for the aliens!

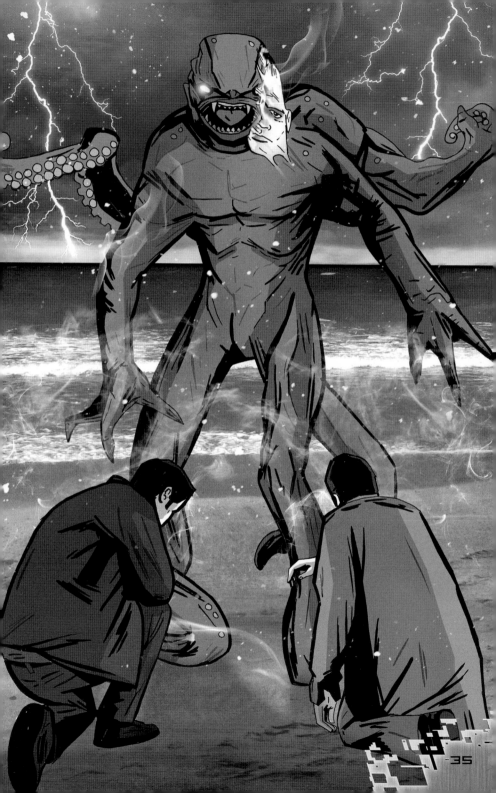

Matt was scared. He had seen too much. He had to get away before anyone found him. As he ran he worked out a plan.

Matt let himself into the empty hotel and packed his bag fast. He grabbed some car keys from reception and drove back to the city. His head was spinning as he tried to make sense of what he had seen.

'What have I been doing for the last few months? Why didn't I see this coming?' he thought. 'I'll pretend I got back to the city earlier on today. Then I can wait and see what they do next.'

It wasn't much of a plan, but it was the best Matt could do. He dumped the car in an alley and ran inside his flat without being seen.

CHAPTER 4

The next day, Matt was back at Sam's cafe. He sat in the shadows. 'Coffee please, Sam,' he said.

'Extra hot with an extra shot?' asked Sam. Matt just nodded.

'Are you ok?' said Sam. But Matt did not hear him.

THE FIRM KEEPS THE WORLD SAFE

He was looking at the TV screen. He could not believe his eyes. The news report was all lies. It was the same in the newspaper. The news said Dexter was a hero. It was a cover up. The Firm was good at that.

Matt knew that the people of the town had done nothing wrong. They had just wanted to live in peace. Nobody there was hiding The Enemy. There was no bomb factory by the sea. Suddenly it all became clear. The Firm was going to give the world over to the aliens. Human life would be over.

Matt knew he had to do something to stop them.
One way or another he needed to find Jane.
They had to save the world.

QUIZ

1. Where did the tip off say The Enemy were hiding?

2. Was Matt pleased to be working with Dexter?

3. What is the name of Matt's missing girlfriend?

4. What advice did Dexter give Matt about his girlfriend?

5. How did Dexter treat the people of the small town?

6. How did Matt react to Dexter's treatment of those people?

7. What did Matt decide to do about his job?

8. What did Dexter and others from The Firm do on the beach?

9. What warning did the alien give?

10. How did Matt get back to the city?

GLOSSARY

cover-up – trying to hide a mistake or crime

coward – someone who is scared to do dangerous or difficult things

know the script – understand the part he is supposed to play

Plan B – back-up plan for when the first plan goes wrong

reception – front desk at a hotel or other public place

tip off – sharing secret information

traitor – someone who betrays the side they are on

ANSWERS

1. The seaside

2. No, they don't get along

3. Jane

4. To forget about her

5. Badly, he bullied them and accused them of lying to The Firm

6. He was angry and walked away

7. Give it up

8. They killed all the people in the town

9. Anyone who tried to hide the Enemy would be killed and the planet would soon belong to the aliens

10. He stole a car

CASE FILE

AUTHOR NAME
Paul Blum

JOB
Teacher

LAST KNOWN LOCATION
London, England

NOTES
Before The Crash taught in London schools.
Author of *The Extraordinary Files* and
Shadows. Believed to be in hiding from The
Firm. Wanted for questioning. Seems to know
more about the new ice age than he should ...

THE MATT MERTON MYSTERIES

Available in bookshops or from <u>risingstars-uk.com</u>

For more information call 0800 091 1602